THE GEORGIA POETRY PRIZE

The University of Georgia Press established the Georgia Poetry Prize in 2016 in partnership with the Georgia Institute of Technology, Georgia State University, and the University of Georgia. The prize is supported by the Bruce and Georgia McEver Fund for the Arts and Environment.

A Season

A Season

Poems

Michael Joseph Walsh

The University of Georgia Press
Athens

Published by the University of Georgia Press
Athens, Georgia 30602
www.ugapress.org

Designed by Melissa Buchanan
Set in Arno Pro
Printed and bound by Integrated Books International

The paper in this book meets the guidelines for permanence and durability of the Committee on Production Guidelines for Book Longevity of the Council on Library Resources.

Most University of Georgia Press titles are available from popular e-book vendors.

Printed in the United States of America
30 29 28 27 26 P 5 4 3 2 1

Library of Congress Control number: 2025947112
ISBN (paperback): 9780820375526
ISBN (epub): 9780820375533
ISBN (PDF): 9780820375540

Contents

A Season

Toccata and Fugue for the Foreigner

Even M must go.
So W reminds himself of his creature as so far created.
W? But W too is creature. Figment.

—SAMUEL BECKETT

내꿈을지배하는자는내가아니다.

I am not the ruler of my dreams.

—YI SANG

Yesterday goes forth from this moment. As a test of our astonishment, a cock crows.

In this body there are head hairs, body hairs, nails, skin, teeth.

Rejection on the one hand, inaccessibility on the other.

The foreigner calls forth a new idea of happiness: smear of light at horizon's commissure, a pantomime of stone lacking flesh.

And how better in the end with leastening words to replace itself.

The psychotic ghost that haunts poetry is the hidden inclusive world.

As if dying instantly, the room organized itself around the angle of my head, my presumed line of sight. I was so at peace I didn't even sneeze. I thought of opium, the front part of the room, its little nip of sun. I thought about the multiplication and breeding of "virtue." Was that evidence of my recovery? The nights took a long time to arrive in those days. Once, holding a familiar knife, the barber lifted my chin, and I felt like a photo of a man stretched out across some train tracks. The sun crawled out from under the blinds, as if to help me remember my life. It felt a little like crying in bed.

Can one be a foreigner and happy?

That whirlwind translates into shrill laughter.

Mountains ride on clouds, mountains walk in the sky.

Painting a decayed tree and polishing a brick of dead ash: we quarrel over the words, our never having come into them.

Or else we remain focused on the phenomenon of origination with regard to the body: whether the door is opened, whether the door is closed.

After that I wanted a long, sound sleep. The deleted phantasms of hope and ambition were jogging up a long bare alley. It was a challenge to rein them in. It was like we were children, trying to counterfeit ourselves. I walked at a leisurely pace. I relaxed my body until my legs were two columns of text on a page, until I was so at peace I could hardly bear the weight of it. That night I watched the sun go down on glass, steel, marble, money, ink. Everything right there, burning up in front of me. I smelled the earth for the first time, then, like others might.

In order to make up from whole cloth an identity, I stand up from my worktable. A spring wind rises.

That all-inclusive wind where words foment: that must indeed be called a beyond.

In those days I worried that I might think myself out of myself, and these thoughts dropped their shadows into both my life and my work. I thought of them like fish: I attended to them, to their smells. "Life is self-providing," I thought, "it's painful to be alive." For a long time after that I sat alone, shivering. The occasional shrill scream from the train, a blank mess of stars in a sky like a burning Void: I don't remember much else, at least not in the usual way. There were four of us at that point, whirling around in tight correspondence. We pulled the quilt back over us, and it was like the moon sinking back into a mackerel cloud.

Let us lighten that otherness by constantly coming back to it.
The mass of suffering wounds him, but in flashes.
When lying down, he discerns, "I am lying down."
The eyeball thunders, crushing the vast sky.

"Is it morning or evening?" I would ask. Life was one long poem in that sense, always ready to explode into laughter. I would fall asleep luxuriously in the moments between blinks, feeling clean, even when I wasn't. When all was said and done it was like applying another lash of the whip to a running horse. As both author and persona I slept soundly, having been a main player even in the depths of my sickness. The rain picked up, the wind picked up. I could hardly believe there could be dreams this vivid. "No one expects to control their dreams," I thought. The earth crumbled beneath me, then, and I laughed a laugh I could feel with my hands.

It is too far buried in the sand.

Initially it is a shock, something unusual, astonishment. You halt with bowed head on the verge of the ditch.

It was as if we had dressed in it: that torrent.

But what does not shake us to our foundations is no mystery.

After that the horizon seemed closer. I played with a magnifying glass, I played with a mirror. I was remote from poetry and willing to feel anything. I went outside, and it was a glorious noon, the kind in which nothing is ever forgotten, nothing digested. "Pleasure, pleasure," I thought, until I found myself engrossed in it. After a while the light split open, rainbowed out its entrails, and I stood and stared until I was left with the feeling that I'd thought the wrong thought, that without meaning to I'd invited the devil in. For days afterward I felt numinous, and a little evil, and sleepy for no reason at all.

Taking up a flower and smiling, without speech.

We call it the moon in terms of properties.

And this body, too, a moment of mountains, rivers, embedded in the flesh of its speaker.

Iridescent skin, refined nostrils.

To pierce the skull of the world and just to sit, as the clash of planes gives rise to a body linked to that "other scene."

This moment of flowers, arrival of flowers.

This primordial, pleasing, death-bearing hand, all white and pupil along invisible blanks.

Even then the panic was just another point beside the main point, the non-point. A few particular people would creep into my periphery and hang there, right where a person's head would be, but never for very long. "There's no accounting for taste," I thought. I wanted to abandon everything. I simpered, I played at vulnerability. Even in my sleep I was like a doll in a music box: there I'd be, facing myself, just a flawless pair of eyes, while the night sky waved like a sea of roiling handkerchiefs. "Good-bye," I'd say, "good-bye," letting the words glisten like oil and spread across my face.

Walking beyond and walking within, he applies it to this very body: a para-thinking, an erotics.

As at that time, at the edge of this, the rumor was: the blood, the dancers, your moon-like form crusted over with translated men.

These bare windows, converging. This great silence evening and night.

In this body there is the earth property, the liquid property, the fire property, and the wind property.

Those deep blue creatures saying "Good friend," writing the words on the forehead and round the corners of the mouth.

I woke up feeling nervous and disoriented, thinking musically. Is this what it means to panic? I tried to imagine what it would feel like to reflect everything: the incredible red, with the green and blue. "It's all a matter of technique," I thought. I'd take the best of my dreams and grind them into poems, potential friends. Driving home it occurred to me that it's important to resist the urge to beautify, if that's what the situation requires. I can say now that I felt better as a result. Life whirled around amid the commotion. The sky blinked open for an instant, and I immediately felt sandy all over my skin.

One can vary the metaphors. Just one straight rod of iron reaches this thing and that.

And the heart: perhaps he crushes me because I negate him.

That the words, the smiles, the manias, the judgments, the tastes of the native are excessive, faltering, or simply unjust and false: he cannot imagine.

On a lower level, on the border between soma and psyche: day and night, awake, confounding.

It is as if I had done nothing, for it is outside myself, in the present but resting on the fossilized remains of a past life.

Not to be precise, not to move.

It is immediately internalized as part of the organism.

This centrally irradiated growth is a fist crushing the empty sky, dripping blood into syllables rekindled at journey's end.

Always mindful, he breathes in; mindful he breathes out.

Wherever the eye reaches gives the same pattern: here a rib, there a breastbone, here a shoulder bone, there a neck bone, here a jaw.

In those intervals of reflection all returns of the repressed are plausible, acceptable, and pleasurable.

"Wouldn't that be something," I thought, "after all this time?" But that was it, that was life in the afternoon: a sense of paralysis, of the body locking up. It was like being in a house of mirrors in which every face is perpetually on its way, and it was pleasurable, deeply pleasurable. I was a person, a personality. I had a particular history and an audience in mind. "A self needs an audience," I thought. "A self is a season." After that I wrote down my thoughts in the order in which they occurred. I swallowed a lot of water, I was proud and ashamed of my pride. I heard the sounds of cars, of helicopters and the like, and for a while the world was sodden, but beautifully so, and life was an exorcism seen through to the end.

I sent tidings to a star, away off there at the break of something.

In the watercourse lay the space that wrecks our abode.

Its journey is the entire body going on the path where no bird flies.

However his body is disposed, that is how he discerns it: fully intimate, half intimate.

Wherever the eye reaches, there is need to make a human chain.

Eventually it was so clear even I could see it: the sliding door dividing the room in half symbolized my destiny. "Does it follow," I wondered, "that there are no happy extremes? Is there anything worse than wind?" I had only one reader, an ideal one, and over time it got easier, calling his bluff. Once I told him "No," and turned around, and I could feel his pending response creep up the back of my neck. Even then, the beauty remained: the sun had a way of exploding open, like a plan for a life. The promised rain would arrive like a stranger's wink, and I would stand there for hours afterwards, wondering if it was meant for me.

The wind begins to rock the grass. The valley sounds are the long broad tongue.

Whatever you dream up entangles an absence, a still life.

A strange light shines on that obscurity that was in you: the operation of the lungs, the digestive system.

We thus stand firmly, facing each other, with bits and pieces of red heart, an iron tree.

Life must be the bird and life must be the fish.

The involution of the strange in the psyche, or the shape of the mountains below it.

"Do you know what personality is?" I said. "It's when you want something so badly the rest of you can't unwant it." Thinking about that made something in me snap, but even that had its precision. It was like lunging into a kiss. I saw depths again, I saw horizons. By night my eyes opened slightly in a way that suggested history, and it was good to know that I had one, a history. Life was a diorama, as it was meant to be, and there was something both attractive and repellent about it—the way everything in hindsight made a story, piercing the snow.

What words for that then?

My memories of experiences when I had been abandoned, perched among words, overwhelm me.

How almost they still ring, they who are companions, movement.

The vast sky does not hinder the vast sky.

My memories at this point were dreams, or nearly dreams, each a pretty doppelgänger of the other, and all crouched adorably as if about to pounce. Life was more engaging now that it was filled with little dangers, and in that sense even nausea was a pleasure: it was a posture, as sentiment is a posture, and in the end in the cloudless dark it was mine, it belonged to me. I was lulled, delighted. I heard the first drops of rain, which neither filled me with agony nor relieved what was there, and I kept an eye on everything, especially on how I felt. It was like looking at myself from behind. After a while I no longer needed it, the foreboding smile of that specter in the glass, so I took a long break from the mirror. So long as my face stayed unreflected it was flushed, prismatic. I tracked all the beautiful birds with their asymmetries reversed, clucking my tongue with pleasure as each rose up and passed away. I had externalized my demons, aestheticized them. I was my own little pet in utero.

Because all moments are the time-being

A paste of flowers spread sloppily across
The soles of the feet

No mystery

The world in those days kept its implied eye covered, though I could feel it wide open behind every intention. I ran through the snow, the driving wind; I watched the clouds clutch softly at the structures of their limits. It was a way of getting started, of widening and growing dark, and every evening as I walked I would disappear into a sunset of my own emotions, flexing in balanced step with the wind. I took careful note of what fixed itself, what didn't, and as this process opened out a kind of shriek unfolded, a shriek that provided, thank God, its own music. It was the earth, in the end, that shriek, irradiating the present like a myth of flowers, and so long as that music played I felt myself as I was, as the continuous end of a story to which there was no end.

Both blossoms and fruits maintain moments: they are a commotion.

You dye the white cloud within the blue sky.

In the wanderer's insane stride toward an elsewhere, blue, yellow, red, and white are mind.

Intimacy renews intimacy, and unleashed eroticism is obliged to resort to new limits: those of organs, which then falter.

Furthermore, just as a skilled butcher or his apprentice, having killed a cow, will sit at a crossroads cutting it up into pieces, so the foreigner's face burns with happiness, precisely knuckled down where the faces of a boat join.

I crawled into bed feeling soggy, and blurry in that way. By then I knew from experience that there was nothing else I could do. My own face, I realized, was reflected in my constellation of needs, and when I closed my eyes I could see it there floating in front of me, glowing and covered in spikes. "Even a place like this," I thought, "is a story that's always ending," and when I finally rose from bed I felt odd, like I'd been bullied. I'd been so naïve. The air was wet, the sky was dark. I hung my head out the window and watched two birds trace their giant arcs in front of me, suggesting the word "Yes" with a preternatural intensity, and as they disappeared slowly into my mind's upper pool my hum of satisfaction deepened into a cautionary roar. I was "awake," at this point, somewhere between laughing and crying, and for a long time after that there was no telling where I'd be. "Where am I," I'd ask, over and over, until I realized that wondering's not always wanting to know, and then I watched as that permission spread over everything: a pestilence, sweetly corrupting, with tendrils that flapped like white tongues in the wind.

The entire body is a mouth: I call it a red furnace.

Such words are less the sign of a thing than of my distrust for them: fleshless skeletons smeared with blood, connected with tendons.

From live metaphor to dead metaphor, with the blood of the finger or the tongue: the inner work of the prosthesis resonates differently in our individual bodies.

We feel the pulls of the different media: fan and mirror, blossom and fruit.

They ring in the flesh for myriad miles.

Eventually I had to admit that in returning to my dreams so often I was only looking for company that was the same as being alone. I had no telos, I'd given up thinking. I watched as one by one my pasts twirled back to face me, until I finally understood that I was myself the camera, that my memories' creations were destined to be my own. "Snap," I said, to make it official. After that I was whole, flush with my viewfinder, and I spent what felt like days turning that feeling over in my mind's eye like a pig on a spit. The wind was howling; the stars were volatilely arranged. To get to sleep I'd close my eyes and imagine myself as a prelude to an exorcism, watching the world fold out into a maelstrom of wire and wood. A sheet of light spilled out of the sky one morning, and I was never the same again. I was petrichor, an apparitional surge. I was a clay head stuffed with flowers in the center of a still pool.

We arrive at the concept grey, the grey point.

We kill space and give light to space.

In this body there are kidneys, liver, pleura, tendons, heart, spleen, and lungs.

This was the soil it grew in, this the hour it bloomed.

Whenever I encountered those stories, I missed them. Had I been wrong to push through? It was like that relief you feel when whatever else you could be doing—rocking from side to side with your eyes rolled back in your head, say—when even that, unearthly or not, starts to bore you. And so I wandered, I drifted. I roamed here and there like a corpse incompletely exhumed. I was shapeless then, a real modern boy, and I marveled at the ruthlessness with which my dreams broke open into their own smiling replacements. I tagged this feeling "seed-burst," "pink leaf." The world unfolded and continued to unfold. It looked at me, smiling, then looked away, still smiling, and all the while I felt calm, correct somehow, like a tightly pulled drum. My eyes buzzed, my head swelled. My hair moved weirdly in some kind of wind.

But is it to be kept up long, this science?

It gets to be an old story: this thing and that thing, with leaves as with fruits and woods.

There must be a certain meagerness of details, a nakedness, as ill-ease with the continuous presence of the utterance of names gives back—with respect to objects and states—that "separate" lucidity the community's function is to erase.

And it is exactly this sound we hear when we are assailed by the strange.

That way go the flames with wild delight, making the outlines of your shadow more distinct.

When walking or standing, talking or remaining silent, you feel the movement in your fellow beings of those inner systems of equipment.

There is walking in the feet, mechanics in the hand.

There is a chain of beginnings that is felt, at least, if not seen.

And just as a dead specimen minutely described re-opens into living figment, so the sun reflecting out in ripples from a flat stone becomes an extravagant speaking out, another dark whose radius grows from the inside out to become the flesh of interior space.

After a while I felt the need for some new mine to ore, some new bone to worry, and the deeper I sank into myself the more piercing it became. I would stand outside for hours watching the sky pass through every possible transformation of dusky color and light. In one sense the spirit behind this was a religious one; in another it was almost lewd. One night in a dream I felt I could breathe underwater so long as I kept my mouth near the surface, and something in the dream implied that anyone could do this, if they would only try. I was sprawled out in bed in a parody of relaxation, the whole touching scene pinning me down where I lay. I was hungry, likely, but not consciously so. Everything was worth remembering.

But those shocks were only for the conscience, only to be produced by opening and protruding the lips.

In that throb of denotation, in that stillness steeped in the warm hum of signs, each intimate other goes beyond understanding.

So confusion too is company, and therein only are you whole and entire.

Farewell to farewell is translated from earth to heaven, and you are shown what you have attained: the flesh, hands and feet, head and eyes.

But then from away behind in that perfect dark foreknell an intimation of the darkness of the original rushes back to make its report:

> "These things occur as the seasons revolve.
>
> You are as you always were:
>
> between what no longer is and what will never be,
>
> the barest gist, alone, bent with a passion that
>
> although tenacious, is only a given, inherited form,
>
> but one that of all the others imaginable
>
> has the most to offer for company."

There was something baptismal about it, that sense of descending into a cold womb and re-emerging an hour later feeling clean somehow, clean and loose. Like a diver having gone too deep who sprints back to the surface, then erupts from the water gasping and relieved: the permission you gave yourself was part of the charm. You clapped your hands together, as if brushing off dirt. What someone said was "sick" or "sickening," a given proposal was "vile," etc. The leaves on the tree outside the window were slightly but evenly wet, so that they seemed almost frosted in the afternoon sun. Smell of fish, smell of waste water, smell of soap. And then it really did open up—a dwelling-place, a cave, a labyrinth that had been deep within me yet unknown. I lay flat on my back with my legs splayed, making good on this chance to rest. I bucked my hips, my muscles locked. The breath of autumn was vast again, its tiny claws dug harshly into my thighs. This was the weather of the day, over time the weather of a life. It was hypnotic, measured, a slow pirouette into madness. I felt attended to, then—surrounded. I loomed over everything like a monstrous crane.

At this you lose your composure.

You feel "lost," "indistinct," "hazy."

An imperative that crumbles in the directions of egg and death produces in you, in the clear twilight, a ghostly world in which those eyes, those lips, those cheek bones, that skin unlike others drift away as if to relieve your attachment to lost space—to flowers overhead, stars underfoot.

And it is with the help of that sole support that you attempt to live.

Thinking is realized, beyond thinking is realized; the boundaries of the actual rustle in a thin cold breeze.

And then, after a day or two, those petals drop off, and new buds open. Manifesting mountains, manifesting streams.

The mind is rightly famous for those winds.

It was like I'd trapped myself with that way of speaking. February was a face that never changed color, and I was bathed in it, neck-deep in it. From my bed I watched my room fold in and out with the wash of my thoughts. I took comfort in that, in that systole of silence and symptom by which one dream recalled another. And wasn't that blessing the one I'd requested? I'd been standing on the other side of the room, short of breath and very alive, and when I'd gone to pick up my head it was there, a porcelain skull. I was pink with blue lips and blue rings around the sockets. Outside it was dreary again, wet but mercifully warm, and thus the season declared itself. I covered my walls with masks and paintings. I continued to live as a human being.

Occurrent beings revealed in breaking down are like stars in the east.

When for relief from outer and inner dark they close and open respectively, the foreigner feels "completely free."

"Because at the start I may myself be chaos," he thinks, "the words are meant to drink us up."

This is making room for another; this is encountering what is rare to encounter.

It is only out of the light, or the gloom, I should say, of their commotion, that the words emerge from the inarticulate, that is, from we know not where.

Breathing in long, you discern, "I am breathing in long," letting intimacy surround you as the hand of the self.

Between fugue and origin the second person marks the voice, from face to face, with the face revealed.

And so it is with the "foreign" languages of bile, phlegm, and blood: the vegetable juices swell gradually into the perfect leaf, bent with a passion that constitutes my translation, my second growth.

Its excess spills out as excrescence, as emergence oozing from the measured earth, and over and over the noisy movements of the clouds, those little sheaves of the right throbs and the wrong, defer all action, and you do nothing.

Nature strews her nuts and flowers: senses and thoughts that are like objects, even weapons, murmuring now and then, "Yes, I remember."

There is a wind in the heart, a fragrance of milk.

There are a parent and a child who are born at the same time.

"Whose voice is this?," you ask, as your movement in relation to breathing bewitches the sunless presence of such a border.

Sometimes a single and causal thought arises, and thus the dream is called the dream: such is its nature, such is its future, such is its unavoidable fate.

Even if you have a good finger to grasp space it remains a mere murmur, picked at by crows and vultures and forever poring over that invisible and promised territory, the words which are its upcurved flesh.

Eight hundred times in the evening you attempt to live with others, and nothing in the sky will distract you.

You cease, all ceases.

You watch as that strange boat takes over the functions of the thing it symbolizes: the corpse of a greater language stretched out across invisible wires.

And yet I welcomed it, strangely, the sense I had that the story could all at once fade quietly out of existence into a wisp of narrative air. I'd get up to pee and return to bed, still half a creature of the dream. Or else I'd remember my taste for blood, which I found had never left me. The smell of cut grass, lucidity, the cloud. I would bob in and out of the dream of the poem, I would feel the heat of the flames on my face. Everyone traded stories about an impressive yellow sunset that in my quarantine I'd somehow missed: a mound of buttered popcorn, soft, prismatic, then a green night sky shaggy with violet stars. I had the feeling then that anything could happen, that wild floodgates had opened. Every night as I slept I felt my body rise up through what felt like hot sand, and every morning the horizon was pliant and quaking, like the skin or the muscles of the abdomen. I was convinced then, deeply, that this was knowledge of vital importance. I was song, pantomime, song, slow fire. And whenever I closed my eyes I saw scores of old friends whom for years I'd not thought of but whom, it turned out, I still loved.

There are also those who transcend, who apply this splitting of the syllables to the body itself.

This we call exhaustive realism, this technē unbinding the heart.

Twice a deformity becomes in that sense a beauty, and it kills you by inches: those ghost leaves, those green ones that in repeating your voice do more than double it.

You thought you had put such things behind you, but within you hear the sound of bells, not nibbling and swallowing merely, but re-making one another in the dark.

Is it sound? or is it form? or is it scent? or is it flavor?

The thing must lie a little remote to be described.

From eye to eye, with the eye held open, you come to know the dark flux of your moods as that element into which your figure disappears.

This autumn, then, is indeed a spring, though we cannot guarantee the permanence of this relief.

You see billions of blossoms, countless blossoms.

You see those flames consuming their natural food.

A Season

L'Étranger? L'Étrange-je.

—EDMOND JABÈS

Me is an I that I proclaim.

—CLARICE LISPECTOR

◆

When for company one has one's body.
Its center filled up with the desire to see.

The desire to see
Everyone
Gradually which is how I was made.

A still flower, floating
Laughing and crying the horizon of rest.

And then after a while the self protests
Hypoxia, notices you falling asleep.
Then passes by way of the flood

From knowing by nothing
To experience, what was there, what I could
In the unfairness of it drive into the nose.

And this panic the world could sustain
Bowed, broken comfort, the splash
Of each misting wave.

As accordingly when I was eyes, and sun, slamming
(Whether I meant to or not).
As accordingly when I re-emerged,
Gasping on the surface by a nearly perfect hill.

And then on went time, on down the days,
In the bare and bleached crust of the earth
The ominous cool of the dream.
And that was it though I hardly trusted it

Chewing attention while the wind slapped my hood.
And the air all pollened, everywhere
At the limit of structure a carapace
In the weather's infrequent promise.

And then the oddly bloodless purple of each
Available feeling tried on then tossed away.

◆

As if the you at work were real, and waiting.
As if on cue for the feeling of what
Happens to me to pull open
Then gently shut.

And be it more than enough
In dark-charged focus in the movie
Theater writhing what I was
In revelation.

What the floodgates
After all, of every itself
That with astonishment propels itself along
Into the footfalls of what would occur—

Better than thought
That life that happens
In what for me rising up
By the thousands is

Material
Vivid with plots of escape.
And night by night the eyes, sudden with breathing.
And day by day what else

Could plausibly be there,
The simple shapes
Of pleasure
Repeating what sounds to me like

"I ate the flower, I ate the flower"
Between rain-wet stones.
Between the practiced
Trajectory of

At intervals this regular me.
Unsated in cold
Water   And not
The by and by—to resolve

Into autonomy,
Into an enormous ray
Of sunlight
Which is the buzz of coming back online.

◆

There it is, we imagine it
In whatever space between trinkets.
Then disgusted again the nested infinities—
One's body one's thoughts—

Or the particular charm of the double
Human a structure of wood.
And I talked to it
As though peering half-naked around a bathroom door

(Which at the time seemed so important)—
A musical thinking, a face
To help remember, a face
Sourced equally at the speed of thought.

And out of the wind the sun,
Then less of it, by brutal
Hum the underpass reflecting all night
In memory all my dreams.

And I could feel the energy of that
Permeating space, that something
Sound I tried to command
Into sense to make anything happen.

Feeling actual, feeling wise, feeling
At the mouth of unnatural experience
The pleasure of relief (release).
As if the sun were alive, the flower-

Made world to be swallowed
Into mind
(Thinking body, thinking mind,
Thinking body) defiant,

In the end possessed by no
Particular endearment
Then new again
In dark carved beginning

Like a house swarmed with love and
Promise (come in or out).

◆

For weeks the same mysterious sadness.
Not every day, but all around.
Of being taken to the hospital alive.
Of speaking so softly as to rarely be heard.

A leaking voice, an hour
As brutally compelling as
A house fire or
A tsunami rolling slowly into shore.

That is how the day begins
With an impression as bad as the sea.
And the sounds the walls feel, sounds
More openly yourself than any

Person scattered
In sudden bloom.
But then very suddenly you sleep.
You are in a clearing, time

Comes flush with the dimples you've carved
In your composite path.
And in this richest of soils unwinding suddenly
Back into sleep you dream

A cognitive music
Flares up at intervals,
You dream
The way teeth dream and stones

Of the particular forces from which you are made.
Then of the people you love
And have forgotten but will remember,
And then of the floodgates opening

In your mind's mouth:
Of wires in bruised orbit,
Of roses
And a room to receive them, the dream

Bestowing its powers and shaping
Like a snake the swallowed world.

◆

What word is there for that.
What wonder clear as this.
To be woundable finally decayed
Into the literature of all soils.

To remember next the rain, the houses
The character of
The morning seeming closer
In a language you don't know

While the water runs
Red its slow passage
In the bowels of feeling with every burst
Feeling more and more

Some shadow, semi-snow—
And behind me
What I meant to express
In the arms of the promised rain,

That things return, the same, that that
Which we have always remained
With eyes, and mouth and hands,
Is the thought that thought would believe—

Mouthing no and frightened yet still
Under shadow,
Is the shock of a perfect heartbeat bearing down.

◆

But how did you do it
At night tied down astonished
And let the surf exhale on your face.
A mess of stars a breath of vast rushed love.

And all your history
Slumped weirdly between brain and heart.
February and
Cowardice the purple watched suspension

Of a sunset that lasts for hours.
In mythic distance.
In a mouth of needles.
The fruit glowing blue against what

Substance, the correlate of leaves.
In the window the electric air
Extracting value from its first pressing.
And then I said to myself, I thought

Having touched a great evil
Having passed over a tangle of sweetgrass, I wondered
And ran on having in turn been made happy

Above the action still floating
In cold weird beauty the blue autumn light—

And at what immaculate odds
Having primed the mind for a world
In process incompletely alive

But also childlike, gentle, sweet
Through the first real stirrings of rain
In sprung life my absence roaring up
Into a halo a throat of gauze.

And this to let the walls be walls, at the edges
Wounded slightly made productively sad.
And the flowers too, screaming
Into steel-blue gradients

Is a job you have to do,
Its bad implied permission
At the edge a still creature nesting in empty space—
Feeling wrong, enlivened,

Feeling itself the subject of a wire-
Like surface—A thinged prose,
Its mouth and eyes—
And at what immaculate odds.

◆

How hard it was then
As an already speechless person
To see the lilies open
With friendliness out of the shaking earth.

As the hummingbird translated from open to open
Is falsely loved, feared and sought, is the rare thing itself
To find the fading line of its knowing

Who enters it and how
That semi-light coupling in space grows bigger

So all the while that slow fury inside you asks
In the burn of blown snow where the heart lives
What tongue describes it what chicken's
Survival does it fear and seek.

In open-book
Apocalypse lost in the light and dangerous
A low roar   In which your whole body turns

Seeing nowhere else, in which the walker
Does not too curiously observe particulars,
Swinging from leaf to leaf
Into ugliness redeeming freedom.

And in that instant abstraction is killed
In the same dark as its creature or in
The most disagreeable kind of snare I never
Before allowed the grotesqueness of,

Writing promise into space and space
Into ribbons, into curtain calls stabbing the air.

◆

And that was spring
Having nothing in it but its own threads
Nor yet unmixed with the previous night's dream—
Flower, voice, lightning, air.

As clouds flare up and drop
Meaning perhaps to honor it
The sun into made sleep

The intimate knots of the dream
At speech's edge our weirdly
Live gods in parallel voice—

Just so the room though utterly dark
Smells good, rhapsodes

For hours its enmeshment with
My own concern

My own felt place,
Something mantra something war, something

Flowers in honest erasure of itself
And makes space for the new snow—

As meaning does
Without, perhaps, loving it
Gets behind a page
And blanks

Wonders flowers wonders love
Into skin the shared same
Chattiness
And skin—

Which is the power of story,
Which is the way to continually arrive

In made
Familiarity in dreams of earlier dreams
In which trust is adequate but never total
Of a gently sloping lawn and on it two mannequins

In twirling preternatural life I had thought
The smiling pattern of the body
Of fibers unwinding into
Their own quiet agendas might hold

Me churning the words
In disappointment

Around that precious and tasteless seed.
And that while I lived was normal

And crushing
The step of life at each new chapter's end—

And at the periphery
Contorting with horror and fascination

As if touched with the juice of the lemon
To have read over and over what
One tendril then another makes real—

In truth, all life

In the blue morning's sheen the mouth
No simple ghost.
Having arrived itself from the future.
Having opened that gap to the wind.

◆

We all have our states of fullness
Being splashed with mud and getting wet with water
And all-too-engrossing to permit of any other

Occasional faint wash of music no music
Ankle-deep in the hiss of private ghosts—

As when the half-dream comes
As if to hear us sing again
From zero to space to absolute
Encirclement

No distinctness no pointedness
In ruthless impossible life as we were meant
To climb inside
Life being born swelling nausea swelling life—

Just so there is in what we love
Also a time for wanting
So badly right then
What it was in the eye of the scream

With every inane
Word a little nearer
To discriminant sweetness
Going slowly playing dumb

Out into the dark and
Pensive embroidery
But aware of the sun and spring
Of one glance back made scarce

As a kind of wind,
Of a hand that moves
To see itself blown out across
As in the old days, in waking, and now,

Across some various difference
Into the light that the I pours in.

◆

Or like the sputter one seeks in an original dark
For all that was memory when the horizon appears
And the background changes

And the flowers pronounce themselves
Into copies of slivered sun.

There is no quavering more reliable

In the morning, inflated, artful, into shreds,
In soft green waves on either side the grass

In the meantime but a ghost
Having been dreamed about, perhaps, then forgotten
As a breaker of promises

And badly dividing your wants from unwants
From snow and wind in evocative

Stone addressed equally to
Inevitable futures
Slackening will

To take the place of change
Wherever the eye's surroundings
For this or that unnatural cloud

And gone but gone
Knowing nothing but the love of being talked to, talking back
Setting fire to the woods

From yesteryear to yesteryear
And rolling till it meets the sand

An inflection
As reality, as painless

Collapsible sunlight and
The blossom of the meadow

To which the flavor of my thought corresponds:
Some blanketing, some rim,

Some mid-molt war
In the history of every one of us

In which a green-winged sky, blue-winged sea
In which in tranquil embedded sun the calm throat

Swells, blind and abated
For sad and vacant reasons   for time

And time when the verdant trash
One seeks in an original dark

Makes a turn, not knowing, over and
Over again, some particle

Jarring viscera from stillness
And thinking the hot heart home.

◆

And then as if through accident or age
Dimly seen in the skull
The skull not having eaten in this moment of sheeny dark
Away behind and behind what it means

This feeling out
After explanation
When the shaking abates
And the image wears away

Having survived the first
Wave inside yourself asking
Which was languorous, which unfurling, which

In the far past in the time of its building
In swells of uncertain dust grew large
And soundly reasoned

When the earth dissolved
Under your feet

And you gradually emerged from it to discover
This way of keeping time with yourself

By flower and shadow and dancing click
By a wanted
Day's explosion any sunrise any need—

  Just so desire imagines
  Its blank become thrill
  Licked smooth into languor aching for proof

That I could ever not want, wanting
Just to be fluid a tranquil mask
Or else human and sudden with being
Being sodden and not one's own

A rooted action, echoed soil, a peering
Foam filled up with looking
From end to cradled end.

◆

Is that what this is? The personality
Of everything perceiving, perceived.
The affective
Correlate of the welcome smell of grass

With which all the houses are filled.
Being at once "dead" and alive in empty space.
The whole truth
Of milk and raw honey, the pressed face

Of the sun when the air is filled with mist.
As when like horses
Or a low flying plane the minutes roar past
In answering reflections

And at a distance above the level of the snow you see
Like the sheen of a moving snake the glint-
Ing contours of the mountains, a still music,
An opening

Out of existence welled into future's   flowered past—
Just so with the other shades preserving
The most interesting and beautiful facts
With educated eyes you go

On a path where no conscious nature comes into its own,
As a wrinkled, corpsey thinness, a diamond
Reflecting everything, a tongueless
Self-performance waking

Married in a sharp high wind.

◆

And if you kept it in (To call the room to it)
As when the previous day's events endeared release—

It is perhaps my failure.
It is perhaps all I remember.

Unwavering brattle the bird of every tempest
That as no word had ever holds familiar in all directions.

That ugliness, stone by stone, one's former body lisped
And sputtered

As if it had actually appeared

Holding on screaming as the train hoots
Hoot hoot remarkable to hold up empty space
In a day this cold, so smooth and unworried

In the blue and red of radiant light
Where I go on eating, drinking, chewing
Where I knock the back of my hand against a stone
And call it stability, stability,

Even then
To ask O yes what truth what else
Without light is drunk or squeezed
Into amiable life, a few words

In the morning's stiff
Neck mouthed in earshot
Rising to the surface
Of the mind a voice speaking not to me

But to the agony of birth
Of constant anticipation
Of no day or night I can account for
Called cold, unlike others, called ash

And dirty snow
Feeling ripe for something, as of the lips
A certain opening
Where the human part of dream sinks into risk.

◆

But it is hard to remember
It is not so simple as that
In electric wetness your your my my

Pushing against the wall it was too soon
For the former body
Needing to breathe again much needing flesh

As sonorous as the peeling air
Which loves but will not listen
Which translates the mark of the scar
Without ever understanding what was good

In health or in sickness on the basis now
Of swarming space better muscled better dreamed—

Or else having itself begun to unzip
Into the same dark fragment as
While moving some kiss of warped light

Yielding to weird
Silence about to vomit the sun begins
To see the one thing not yet eaten, a pearl

Plucked from far in the past
Where there was clover growing
A deep shadow
A smile entrained on the border between

This day, yesterday, the dawn
Between structure and sewn story based on I
And this nothing, a sea
Inside me like in no suspended

Thirst the story is
From end to end a natural home

A life-dream crossed with blood
And extra light

To which I'd give myself
In this indirect way
Stretched out in the dark and aware of it
This necessary

Split of flower and fruit
Of summer and strange spring.

◆

One is never too young for history
When the question arrives again.

Every edge written in encouraging nature
And still conscious of sounds in air.

Where there are no trees, living
With resonances, reasonings
Whose linings are gathered in

Into long-walk, meadow-sweet, skin-
Savored somnolence,

Into a warning sun that burns forever
And buzzes like a specter on the lawn

Across the pond's green skin the quiet flash
Of aftermath, no lineament, to make the truer earth

The regular image of a face
Spotted bright with red
Or crimson coarse with wooly white—

Then transforms it into offering
Against the grain, either of the will or the imagination,

Into folded space, theory of horizon,
Impenetrable body returning its almost-loved
Majesty lifted quietly above the level of the real—

And all the more as we dimly sense it in ourselves
That the thrill of it lies in descent, the open hand

Like the leap of a cat in solemn love not understanding
The low hum or susurrus
Of a myriad world's arrangement risk and sun.

And peering at us up from there
In mirrors, in windows, in crowds,
All back in the skull and so akin

And alive at night with the bodies that grow from what
Will be said without your having said it:

Surviving, surviving, what's called keeping up
With one's organism the sound of footfalls

In silence not without pain the slow fur
Of choked-up rage the shaking hand's

Bright comfort in an icy moonscape

Eating and swallowing the lips
As good as war the mantra nearly noise—

So as not to break it, not to see

What this world is, how it might well cease
Inhabited by eggs clay cherubim a life of dreams

As if you had been looking at it for years and known it always
Having touched the bottom beyond which
Pathos struck ceilings arch wakefulness
For which the world afterward deforms

Into everything snatched clear from voice
In the fullness of illumination teetering into the dark
Early morning, in the same breath, renewed
With such fine bold humor and

The mouth half-seen in light of last
Is what you know
In kindred voices

Drawn as I from myself and me
And returning to story, always, as it is,

Into the backwards new world on the line of the horizon
Into the heart like a cool green sea.

Notes

The non-italicized passages of "Toccata and Fugue for the Foreigner" are made mainly of quotations and fragments from the following texts:

Beckett, Samuel. *Three Novels: Molloy, Malone Dies, The Unnamable.* Edited by Laura Lindgren. New York: Grove Press, 2009.

Beckett, Samuel, and S. E. Gontarski. *Nohow On: Company, Ill Seen Ill Said, and Worstward Ho.* New York: Grove Press, 2014.

Blaser, Robin. "Image Nation 5 (erasure)."

Dickinson, Emily. "The Wind begun to rock the Grass."

Duncan, Robert. "A New Poem (for Jack Spicer)."

James, Henry. *Delphi Complete Works of Henry James.* Delphi Classics, 2013.

Kristeva, Julia. *Strangers to Ourselves.* Revised edition. New York: Columbia University Press, 1994.

Nanamoli, Bhikkhu, and Bhikkhu Bodhi, trans. *The Middle Length Discourses of the Buddha: A Translation of the Majjhima Nikaya.* Boston: Wisdom Publications, 1995.

Spicer, Jack. "Radar, A Postscript for Marianne Moore."

Spiller, Jürg, ed. *The Thinking Eye: The Notebooks of Paul Klee.* Translated by Ralph Manheim. First edition. New York: George Wittenborn, 1961.

Tanahashi, Kazuaki, and Peter Levitt, eds. *The Essential Dōgen: Writings of the Great Zen Master.* Boston: Shambhala, 2013.

Thoreau, Henry David. *The Journal of Henry David Thoreau*. Edited by Damien Searls. New York: NYRB Classics, 2009.

Weightman, John. "Language as Prosthesis." *The Hudson Review* 53, no. 1 (Spring 2000): 53–62.

The italicized passages are made mainly of fragments from a personal diary I kept from 2016–2018. They also include a few borrowed or adapted phrases from other sources, as well as more frequent borrowings from Yi Sang, especially the following translation of the short stories "The Wings," "Encounters and Departures," and "Deathly Child":

Yi, Sang. *The Wings*. Translated by Jung-hyo Ahn and James B. Lee. The Portable Library of Korean Literature, Short Fiction 1. Jimoondang Publishing Company, 2001.

The phrase "the continuous end of a story to which there was no end" is adapted from a phrase that appears in "Miss Banquett, or the Populating of Cosmania," a short story by Laura Riding.

The phrase "company that was the same as being alone" is borrowed from "Winter, 1965," a short story by Frederic Tuten that appeared in the Fall 2014 issue of *Bomb*.

"Toccata and Fugue for the Foreigner" is the title of the first chapter of Julia Kristeva's *Strangers to Ourselves*.

The poems in *A Season* occasionally adapt language from all of the above sources, as well as from the following works by Clarice Lispector:

Lispector, Clarice. *Água Viva*. Translated by Stefan Tobler. Edited by Benjamin Moser. New York: New Directions, 2012.

Lispector, Clarice. *The Complete Stories*. Translated by Katrina Dodson. Edited by Benjamin Moser. New York: New Directions, 2018.

Acknowledgments

Thank you to the editors of the *Brooklyn Rail, DIAGRAM, Dream Pop Press, DREGINALD, either/or, FOLDER, mercury firs, Poetry Daily, Pouch, Sink Review,* and *Works and Days,* where some of these poems first appeared.

Thank you to my friends and teachers, with special thanks to John Cotter, Graham Foust, Elisa Gabbert, Aditi Machado, Bin Ramke, Selah Saterstrom, Eleni Sikelianos, and Rod Smith for various forms of help and encouragement.

Thank you to Andrew Zawacki for believing in the book.

Thank you, always, to my family.

THE GEORGIA POETRY PRIZE

Christopher Salerno, *Sun & Urn*

Christopher P. Collins, *My American Night*

Rosa Lane, *Chouteau's Chalk*

Chelsea Dingman, *Through a Small Ghost*

Chioma Urama, *A Body of Water*

Jasmine Elizabeth Smith, *South Flight*

Leah Nieboer, *Soft Apocalypse*

Jessica Tanck, *Winter Here*

Michael Joseph Walsh, *A Season*